SMP 11-16

Book YE1

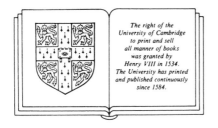

The right of the
University of Cambridge
to print and sell
all manner of books
was granted by
Henry VIII in 1534.
The University has printed
and published continuously
since 1584.

Cambridge University Press

Cambridge
New York   Port Chester
Melbourne   Sydney

Published by the Press Syndicate of the University of Cambridge
The Pitt Building, Trumpington Street, Cambridge CB2 1RP
40 West 20th Street, New York, NY 10011–4211, USA
10 Stamford Road, Oakleigh, Melbourne 3166, Australia

First published 1986
Fourth printing 1991

Diagrams and phototypesetting by Parkway Group, London and Abingdon,
and Gecko Limited, Bicester, Oxon.

Cover illustration by Graeme Portlock

Printed in Great Britain at the University Press, Cambridge

British Library cataloguing in publication data

SMP 11–16 yellow series.
  Bk YE1
  1. Mathematics – 1961 –
  I. School Mathematics Project
  510   QA39.2

ISBN 0 521 31671 5

Contents

1 Finite arithmetics

Introduction

Many people study mathematics because it is useful in many ways. But often people find mathematics interesting in itself, even if they can see no practical use for it.

Although this chapter starts out with a few practical examples, the main purpose of the chapter is not to teach you useful mathematics.

The chapter illustrates one of the ways which new branches of mathematics are invented or discovered. Mathematicians often take a piece of ordinary, well-known, mathematics and ask 'What do we get if we change some of the rules?'

It's rather like taking a well-known game such as chess or draughts and changing some of the rules to make a new game. The new game may be interesting to play; it may also be interesting to compare the new game with the old one.

In this chapter, the 'old game' is ordinary arithmetic with numbers, positive and negative. These numbers can be marked on an infinite number line:

The 'new game' is a **finite** arithmetic, with only seven numbers. The number line becomes a circle.

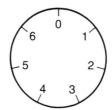

A Days of the week

The days of the week can be numbered like this.

Sun	Mon	Tue	Wed	Thur	Fri	Sat
0	1	2	3	4	5	6

An inspector visits a farm on a Sunday, and after that at
intervals of 3 days.
So these are the days of his visits.

   0   3   6   2
Su M T **W** Th F **Sa** Su M **T** W . . .

A1 (a) Continue the sequence of visiting days 0, 3, 6, 2, . . . until
0 (Sunday) comes round again.

(b) How many weeks are there between the Sunday visits?

A2 (a) Suppose the inspector visits on Sunday and then at intervals
of 4 days. Write down the sequence of visiting days until
0 comes round again.

(b) How many weeks are there between the Sunday visits?

A3 Another inspector visits at intervals of 5 days.
Her first visit is on a Sunday.

(a) Copy and complete this table. It shows the day of the week
for each of her first 10 visits.

Visit	1st	2nd	3rd	4th	5th	6th	7th	8th	9th	10th
Day	0	5								

(b) Use the pattern in the table to work out the day of the
week for   (i) the 29th visit   (ii) the 75th visit

A4 A patient has to take a tablet at intervals of 6 days.
He takes the first tablet on a Tuesday. On what day of
the week does he take the 20th tablet?

B Arithmetic with only seven numbers

The days of the week can be shown on
a 'clockface' with 7 points, like this.

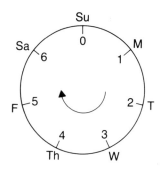

Suppose an inspector visits on day 0 (Sunday) and then at
intervals of 3 days.
You can think of this as starting at 0 and adding 3
each time, provided you think of 6 + 3 as 2.

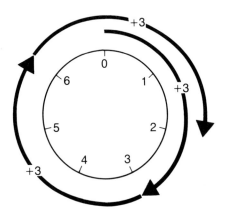

We can do a kind of arithmetic using only the seven numbers
0, 1, 2, 3, 4, 5 and 6.
Here are some sums in this seven-number arithmetic.

$2 + 5 = 0$ (Start at 2; go 5 clockwise. You get to 0.)

$3 + 6 = 2$ (Start at 3; go 6 clockwise. You get to 2.)

B1 Do these. (a) $4 + 4$ (b) $1 + 6$ (c) $6 + 5$ (d) $3 + 2$

The seven-number arithmetic is called **arithmetic modulo 7**.

B2 Copy and complete this addition table for arithmetic modulo 7.

+	0	1	2	3	4	5	6
0	0	1	2	3	4	5	6
1	1	2	3	4	5	6	0
2	2	3					
3							
4							
5							
6							

2 + 1 goes here.

Subtraction

When we add, we go clockwise round the circle.
Subtracting is the inverse of adding, so we can subtract by going **anticlockwise**.

For example, $2 - 4$ could be thought of like this.

We can see that $2 - 4 = 5$.

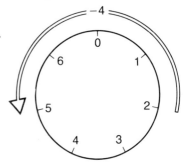

B3 Do these subtractions in arithmetic modulo 7.

(a) $2 - 3$ (b) $5 - 3$ (c) $3 - 6$ (d) $0 - 4$ (e) $1 - 5$

B4 Start at any number and subtract 2. Note the result.
Can you get the same result by starting as before and **adding** something? What number do you add?

Subtraction not needed

This diagram illustrates 2 − 4.
This result is 5.

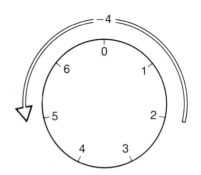

But in fact we do not need subtraction at all.
Instead of **subtracting 4** we can **add 3**.
The result is the same.

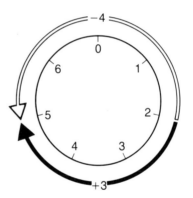

Whatever number we start with, **adding 3** will give the same
result as **subtracting 4**.

+3 (add 3) is called the **equivalent addition** for −4 (subtract 4).

B5 Write down the equivalent addition for

(a) −1   (b) −5   (c) −2   (d) −6   (e) −3

B6 Convert each of these subtractions into an addition, using the
equivalent addition. The first is done for you as an example.

(a) 4 − 5   (b) 2 − 6   (c) 1 − 4   (d) 5 − 2   (e) 2 − 5
= 4 + 2
= 6

Negative numbers not needed

In ordinary arithmetic, negative numbers are needed when a subtraction gives a result which is less than 0.

For example, $2 - 5 = {}^-3$.

But in arithmetic modulo 7, $2 - 5$ is equivalent to $2 + 2$, which is 4. Negative numbers are not needed.

In ordinary arithmetic, the number line is straight.
The positive and negative numbers pair off on either side of zero.

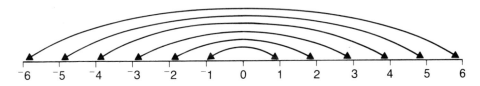

In arithmetic modulo 7, the number 'line' is a circle.
The numbers pair off on either side of zero like this.

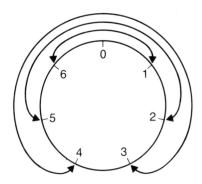

So, for example, 6 does the job of $^-1$.   6 is the 'negative' of 1.

In ordinary arithmetic, when you add a number to its negative you get 0. For example, $1 + {}^-1 = 0$.

The same is true in arithmetic modulo 7. For example, $1 + 6 = 0$.

B7   In arithmetic modulo 7, which number is the 'negative' of

(a) 3   (b) 5   (c) 6   (d) 4   (e) 2

C Multiplication

You can think of 4×3 as either 'four threes' or 'three fours'.
'Four threes' can be worked out in arithmetic modulo 7 like this.

$$\underbrace{3+3}+3+3$$
$$= \underbrace{6 \;\; +3}+3$$
$$= \quad 2 \quad +3$$
$$= \; 5$$

C1 Check that $4+4+4$ gives the same result.

C2 Work out (a) 2×5 (b) 4×5

Another way to work out the answer to a multiplication is this.

Think of 4×3 as $4+4+4$, or better still as $0+4+4+4$.
On the clockface it looks like this.

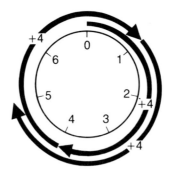

The complete 'journey' takes you once right round the clock and
then on to 5.
This is because $4 \times 3 = 12$ (in ordinary arithmetic)

$$= 7+5 \quad \text{(in ordinary arithmetic)}$$
$$= \text{(once round the clock)} + 5$$

Similarly, $5 \times 4 = 20$
$= 14 + 6$ } in ordinary arithmetic

$=$ (twice round the clock) $+ 6$

So $5 \times 4 = 6$ in arithmetic modulo 7.

C3 Work these out in arithmetic modulo 7.

(a) 4×6 (b) 5×5 (c) 6×3 (d) $3 \times 3 \times 3$

C4 Copy and complete this multiplication table for arithmetic modulo 7.

×	0	1	2	3	4	5	6
0	0	0	0	0	0	0	0
1	0	1	2	3	4	5	6
2	0	2	4	6	1	3	5
3	0	3	6				
4							
5							
6							

C5 What number does **?** stand for in each of these equations in arithmetic modulo 7?

(a) $2 \times \mathbf{?} = 5$ (b) $4 \times \mathbf{?} = 2$ (c) $\mathbf{?} \times 5 = 1$ (d) $\mathbf{?} \times 3 = 5$

Squares and cubes

C6 When you multiply a whole number by itself, the result is called a **square** number. For example, in ordinary arithmetic 64 is a square number because $64 = 8 \times 8$.

Which are the square numbers in arithmetic modulo 7?

C7 When you cube a whole number, the result is called a **perfect cube**. For example, in ordinary arithmetic 27 is a perfect cube, because $27 = 3 \times 3 \times 3$.

Which are the perfect cubes in arithmetic modulo 7?

11

D Division

Here is part of the multiplication table for ordinary arithmetic.

×	0	1	2	3	4	5
0	0	0	0	0	0	0
1	0	1	2	3	4	5
2	0	2	4	6	8	10
3	0	3	6	9	12	15
4	0	4	8	12	16	20

We can use this multiplication table to find the answers to certain divisions, for example $12 \div 3$.

We go along the 3 row in the table until we get to 12.
12 appears in the 4 column, so $12 \div 3$ is 4.

It is worth remembering that $3 \times 4 = 12$, $12 \div 3 = 4$ and $12 \div 4 = 3$ are all ways of saying the same thing.

We can use the same idea in arithmetic modulo 7.

Here is the multiplication table.

×	0	1	2	3	4	5	6
0	0	0	0	0	0	0	0
1	0	1	2	3	4	5	6
2	0	2	4	6	1	3	5
3	0	3	6	2	5	1	4
4	0	4	1	5	2	6	3
5	0	5	3	1	6	4	2
6	0	6	5	4	3	2	1

Suppose we want to do $6 \div 2$.
We go along the 2 row until we get to 6.
6 is in the 3 column, so $6 \div 2 = 3$ (as in ordinary arithmetic).

To do $5 \div 3$, look along the 3 row until you get to 5.
5 is in the 4 column, so $5 \div 3 = 4$.

$3 \times 4 = 5$, $5 \div 3 = 4$ and $5 \div 4 = 3$
are all ways of saying the same thing.

D1 Use the multiplication table for arithmetic modulo 7 to do these.

(a) $3 \div 5$ (b) $2 \div 6$ (c) $6 \div 5$ (d) $1 \div 3$

D2 (a) Copy this table. Complete it by dividing each number by 3 (in arithmetic modulo 7).

(b) You can get the same set of results by **multiplying** by something instead of dividing.

What number do you multiply by?

$\div 3$	
0	0
1	5
2	3
3	
4	
5	
6	

$\times\,?$	
0	0
1	5
2	3

Reciprocals

In ordinary arithmetic, the **reciprocal** of a number is $\dfrac{1}{\text{the number}}$.

For example, the reciprocal of 4 is $\frac{1}{4}$ or $0 \cdot 25$,

the reciprocal of 5 is $\frac{1}{5}$ or $0 \cdot 2$,

the reciprocal of 20 is $\frac{1}{20}$ or $0 \cdot 05$.

When you multiply a number by its reciprocal, you get **1**.

$$4 \times \tfrac{1}{4} = 1 \qquad 5 \times \tfrac{1}{5} = 1 \qquad 20 \times \tfrac{1}{20} = 1$$

Look at the multiplication table you made for arithmetic modulo 7. You should have found that $4 \times 2 = 1$. This means that in arithmetic modulo 7.

4 is the reciprocal of 2 and **2 is the reciprocal of 4.**

D3 (a) To find the reciprocal of 3 you have to find the number which fits the equation $3 \times \textbf{?} = 1$. What is the reciprocal of 3 in arithmetic modulo 7?

(b) What is the reciprocal of   (i) 5   (ii) 6   (iii) 1   (iv) 0

Division not needed

In ordinary arithmetic, **dividing something by 3** is the same as **working out $\frac{1}{3}$ of it**. Similarly, dividing something by 20 is the same as working out $\frac{1}{20}$ of it.

Dividing by a number is the same as **multiplying by its reciprocal**. For example, $60 \div 3$ is the same as $60 \times \frac{1}{3}$ (or $\frac{1}{3}$ of 60).

The same idea works in arithmetic modulo 7.
We have seen that the reciprocal of 3 is 5.
So instead of **dividing by 3** we can **multiply by 5**.

(This explains the result you should have obtained in question D2.)

Division is not needed in arithmetic modulo 7.

D4 In arithmetic modulo 7, what multiplication is equivalent to

(a) divide by 2 (b) divide by 5 (c) divide by 6

D5 Work out each of these in arithmetic modulo 7 by replacing each division by its equivalent multiplication.

(a) $3 \div 4$ (b) $5 \div 4$ (c) $5 \div 6$ (d) $6 \div 5$ (e) $2 \div 3$

Check each answer from the multiplication table. (For example, to check the answer to $3 \div 4$, find the number which fits $4 \times \textbf{?} = 3$.)

Fractions not needed

In ordinary arithmetic, fractions are necessary because some divisions (for example, $5 \div 2$) do not work out as exact whole numbers.

In arithmetic modulo 7, all divisions work out exactly.
For example, $5 \div 2 = 5 \times$ reciprocal of 2
$$= 5 \times \quad 4$$
$$= 6$$

No fractions are needed in arithmetic modulo 7.

E Solving equations in arithmetic modulo 7

Here for reference are tables showing which addition or multiplication is equivalent to each subtraction or division in arithmetic modulo 7.

Subtraction	Equivalent addition
-1	$+6$
-2	$+5$
-3	$+4$
-4	$+3$
-5	$+2$
-6	$+1$

Division	Equivalent multiplication
$\div 1$	$\times 1$
$\div 2$	$\times 4$
$\div 3$	$\times 5$
$\div 4$	$\times 2$
$\div 5$	$\times 3$
$\div 6$	$\times 6$

Here is a very simple equation in ordinary arithmetic.

$$x + 5 = 2$$

To solve the equation, you would **subtract 5** from both sides.

$$x + \underbrace{5 - 5}_{+0} = 2 - 5$$

$$x = {}^-3$$

Now think of the equation as an equation in arithmetic modulo 7.

$$x + 5 = 2$$

You do not subtract 5 from each side. You use the equivalent operation **add 2**.

$$x + \underbrace{5 + 2}_{+0} = 2 + 2$$

$$x = 4$$

E1 Solve these equations in arithmetic modulo 7.

(a) $x + 4 = 1$ (b) $x + 2 = 1$

(c) $x + 6 = 3$ (d) $x + 4 = 2$

Here is another simple equation in ordinary arithmetic.	$2x = 3$

To solve it you would **divide both sides by 2**. Or you could **multiply both sides by $\frac{1}{2}$**, which is the same.	$\dfrac{2x}{2} = \dfrac{3}{2}$ $(\text{or } 2x \times \tfrac{1}{2} = 3 \times \tfrac{1}{2})$ $x = 1\tfrac{1}{2}$

Now think of the equation as an equation in arithmetic modulo 7.	$2x = 3$

You do not divide both sides by 2. You use the equivalent operation **multiply by 4**.	$\underbrace{4 \times 2}_{1} x = 4 \times 3$ $x = 5$

E2 Solve each of these equations in arithmetic modulo 7.

(a) $2x = 5$ (b) $3x = 2$ (c) $5x = 4$ (d) $3x = 4$ (e) $5x = 2$

Here, for comparison, is the equation $3x + 4 = 2$, solved in ordinary arithmetic and in arithmetic modulo 7.

─── Ordinary arithmetic ───	─── Arithmetic modulo 7 ───
$3x + 4 = 2$	$3x + 4 = 2$
Subtract 4 from both sides. $3x + \underbrace{4 - 4}_{+0} = 2 - 4$	Add 3 to both sides. $3x + \underbrace{4 + 3}_{+0} = 2 + 3$
$3x = {}^{-}2$	$3x = 5$
Divide both sides by 3. $x = \dfrac{{}^{-}2}{3}$	Multiply both sides by 5. $\underbrace{5 \times 3}_{1} x = 5 \times 5$ $x = 4$

16

E3 (a) Copy and complete the working to solve this equation in arithmetic modulo 7.

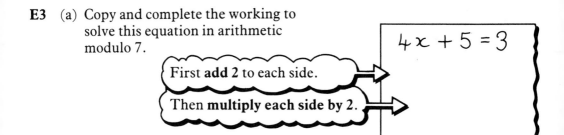

First **add 2** to each side.

Then **multiply each side by 2**.

$$4x + 5 = 3$$

(b) Check that your answer fits the original equation.

E4 Solve each of these equations in arithmetic modulo 7.

(a) $2x = 3$ (b) $2x + 5 = 3$ (c) $3x + 1 = 2$

(d) $4x + 5 = 1$ (e) $5x + 4 = 3$ (f) $6x + 5 = 3$

F Other finite arithmetics

An arithmetic with only seven numbers, or five numbers, or twenty-three numbers, and so on, is called a **finite arithmetic**. Ordinary arithmetic has infinitely many numbers.

F1 Investigate the finite arithmetic which has only the five numbers 0, 1, 2, 3 and 4, in the following way.
(a) Draw a clockface.
(b) Make an addition table.
(c) Make a table showing the equivalent addition for each subtraction.
(d) Make a multiplication table.
(e) List the square numbers and the perfect cubes.
(f) Write down the reciprocals of 1, 2, 3 and 4.
(g) Make a table showing the equivalent multiplication for each division.
(h) Make up some equations and solve them.

F2 Something peculiar happens in the finite arithmetic with six numbers 0, 1, 2, 3, 4 and 5. Investigate.

Problems and investigations (1)

1 Square squares

Reading across in this number square
you get three numbers 256, 144 and 484,
which are all square numbers.

Reading down, the three numbers 214, 548
and 644 are **not** square numbers.

2	5	6
1	4	4
4	8	4

Can you put figures into the square so that the three-figure
numbers across and down are all square numbers?
(Three-figure numbers starting with a 0 are not allowed.)

Can you find different ways to do it?

2 Cross squares

This 'number cross' obeys two rules.

(1) The numbers reading across are the
same as those reading down.

(2) All the numbers, reading across or
down, are square numbers.

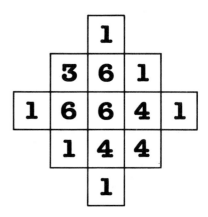

Can you find other ways to fill the cross so as to
obey the two rules?
(Once again, numbers starting with a 0 are not allowed.)

2 Networks

A   Vertices and edges

A network consists of points called **vertices** joined by lines called **edges**.

There may be more than one edge joining two vertices.

An edge may start and finish at the same vertex.

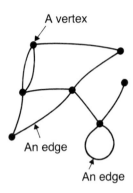

A vertex

An edge

An edge

Networks can be **connected** or **disconnected**. A disconnected network is split up into separate parts, with no edges joining the parts.

A connected network

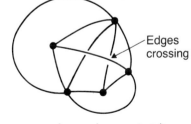

A disconnected network

Networks can be **planar** or **non-planar**. In a planar network, no edges cross over one another.

A planar network

Edges crossing

A non-planar network

All the networks in this chapter are **connected** and **planar**.

Each edge in a network can be thought of as split into 2 'half-edges'. Each half-edge 'belongs' to one of the vertices.

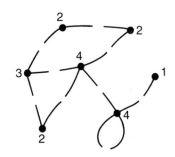

The number of half-edges at a vertex is called the **degree** of the vertex.

The diagram on the right shows a network whose edges have been split into half-edges. The degree of each vertex is shown.

A1 (a) Write down the degree of each vertex in this network.

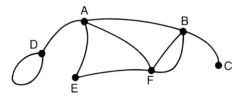

(b) Count the number of edges in the network.

(The answers are on the back page. Check them before you continue.)

A2 (a) Draw a network with three vertices X, Y and Z whose degrees are   X 3,   Y 3,   Z 2.

(b) Count the edges in your network.

A3 (a) Write down the degrees of P, Q, R and S in each of these networks.

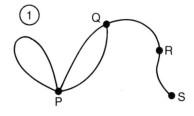
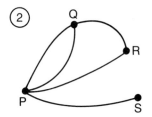
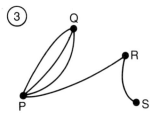

(b) Count the number of edges in each of the networks.

(c) Draw a network of your own with four vertices P, Q, R and S of degrees 4, 3, 2 and 1.

(d) Count the number of edges in your network.

A4 Write down the degrees of the vertices in each of the
networks below. Add up the degrees for each network
and also count the number of edges in it.
Write your results in a table like this.

Network	Degrees of vertices	Sum of degrees	Number of edges
(a) (b)	3, 3, 2, 1, 1	10	5

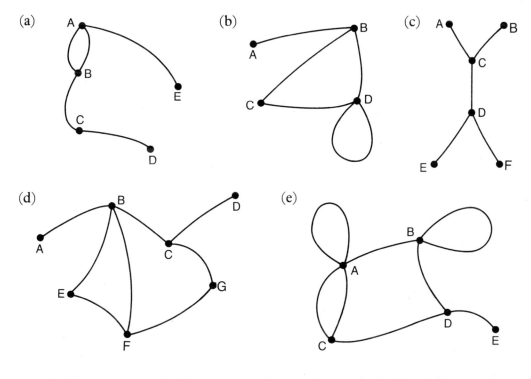

(f) Draw a network of your own and enter the results in the table.

(g) Draw another network of your own and do the same.

A5 (a) Write down the rule connecting the sum of the degrees
and the number of edges.

(b) Explain why the rule must be true for every network.
(**Hint.** The diagram at the top of the opposite page may help.)

The degree of a vertex is the number of half-edges which meet there.

So when you add up all the degrees, you get the total number of half-edges in the network.

To get the number of edges you divide this by 2 because 2 half-edges make one edge.

For example, in the network on the right,

$$\text{Total number of half edges} = 2 + 3 + 4 + 2 + 2 + 4 + 1$$
$$= 18$$

$$\text{Number of edges} = \frac{18}{2} = 9$$

A6 A network has seven vertices whose degrees are 1, 2, 2, 3, 4, 5, 5. Calculate the number of edges without drawing the network.

A7 How can you tell without drawing that it is impossible to draw a network with six vertices whose degrees are 1, 2, 3, 4, 4, 5?

A8 (a) A network has 8 vertices, each of degree 3. How many edges are there?

(b) A network has V vertices, each of degree n. Write an expression for the number of edges.

A9 A network has 24 edges and every vertex is of degree 3. How many vertices are there?

A10 A network has 9 edges and 5 vertices. The degrees of four of the vertices are 1, 3, 4, 4.

What is the degree of the fifth vertex?

A11 (a) Copy this network and write against each vertex the degree of that vertex.

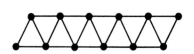

(b) In the network shown, there is a top row of six vertices and a bottom row of six vertices.
Imagine a similar network with 60 vertices in the top row and 60 in the bottom. Calculate the number of edges.

B Trees

The arrows on this diagram show closed paths
or **circuits**.

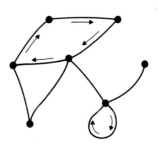

A network with no circuits in it is called a **tree**.

Trees

B1 There are a number of ways of making
this network into a tree by removing
just **one** edge.

Which edge could it be?

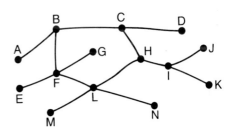

B2 Draw this tree.

Is there anywhere where you can add
an edge joining two of the vertices, and
the new network is still a tree?

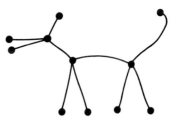

B3 Count the number of vertices and the number of edges in the
tree in question B2.

Draw some more trees of your own and do the same.

Find a rule connecting V, the number of vertices, and
E, the number of edges in a tree.

When a rule has been discovered in mathematics, the next step is to try to find the reason why it is true.

The reason for the rule connecting V and E for a tree lies in the fact that a tree can be built up starting from a single vertex and no edges.

Here is an example of a tree.

The table below shows one way of building up the tree.
The values of V and E at each stage are shown.

V	1	2	3	4	5	6	7	8
E	0	1	2	3	4	5	6	7

B4 Build up the tree above in a different way, starting with a different vertex. Make a table similar to the one above.

B5 Make a similar table for building up this tree. Start with a single vertex and no edges.

From your tables, you should notice two things.

(1) To start with $V - E$ is 1, because V is 1 and E is 0.

(2) At every stage, one vertex and one edge are added.
So V and E both go up by 1 each time.
So $V - E$ is not changed.

It follows that $V - E$ will always be 1 for a tree, because $V - E$ is 1 to start with, and then does not change while the tree is being built up.

B6 The telephone cable problem

A, B, C, D, E, F, G and H are eight towns.
They are to be connected together by a network of
telephone cables.

The connection between two towns does not have to be direct.
It can go through other towns on the way.

The dotted lines show where cables could be laid, and the
cost of each cable is shown (in units of £10 000).

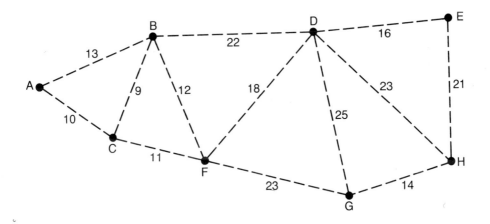

The telephone engineer has to decide which cables to lay,
so as to make the network as cheap to build as possible.

(a) Explain why the network has to be a tree.

(b) How many cables will need to be laid?

(c) Draw a diagram showing the cables which have to be
laid to make the cost as low as possible.

(d) What is the cost of the cheapest network?

B7
A survey of the land between towns D and G leads to a
revised estimate of the cost of a cable from D to G.
The new estimate is 15 units instead of 25 units.

Does this make any difference to the decision as to
which cables to lay?

B8 This is a plan of a farm, which is surrounded by open country. There are animals in every field.

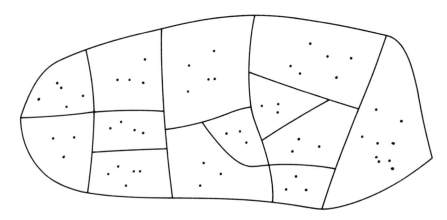

(a) What is the smallest number of fences which have to be broken for all the animals to be able to escape into the open country?

(b) What has this problem got to do with trees?

B9 This object is made from metal links.

What is the largest number of links which can be broken without the object splitting up into separate pieces?

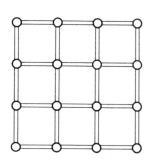

(For example, if you break these two links, the object splits up.)

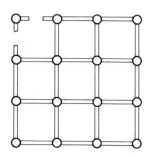

B10 Re-do question B9 for a 10 × 10 grid instead of a 3 × 3 grid.

3 Algebra with a difference

A   A simple robot

The triangular marker in the diagram below represents a
simple robot, which moves along a numbered track.

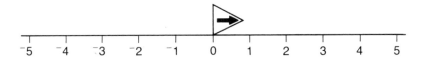

The robot can make two kinds of move.

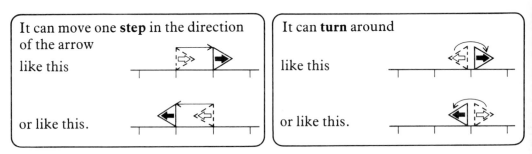

We will use letters to stand for the two kinds of move.
Let *s* stand for 'move one step in the direction of the arrow'.
Let *t* stand for 'turn around'.

A1   The starting position is **at 0, facing right**.

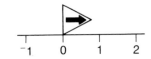

In what position does the marker end up if it does

(a)   *t* followed by *s* followed by *t*

(b)   *s* followed by *t* followed by *s* followed by *t*

It will be useful to have a symbol to mean 'followed by'.
We will use a small circle ∘ to mean 'followed by'.
So *t*∘*s* means '*t* followed by *s*'.

A2 Draw a number line numbered from ⁻5 to 5.
Draw a marker in the starting position at 0, facing right.

For each of these combinations of moves, draw the final position of the marker.

(a) $t \circ s \circ t \circ s \circ s$ (b) $s \circ s \circ t \circ s \circ t \circ s \circ s$ (c) $t \circ s \circ t \circ s \circ s \circ t \circ t \circ s$

A3 With the same starting position as in question A2, say where the marker will be after

(a) $t \circ s \circ t \circ s \circ s \circ s$ (b) $s \circ s \circ s \circ s \circ t \circ s \circ s \circ t$ (c) $s \circ s$

In the last question, you should have found that the marker finishes in exactly the same position for each of the three combinations of moves

They are different combinations of moves, but they all have the same effect. When two combinations have the same effect, we say they are equivalent or **equal** to each other, and we write this using the = sign. For example,

$$t \circ s \circ t \circ s \circ s \circ s = s \circ s \circ s \circ s \circ t \circ s \circ s \circ t$$

The simplest combination of the three is $s \circ s$. It is not possible to find a simpler combination with the same effect.

A4 Find the simplest combination which is equal to each of these.

(a) $t \circ s \circ s \circ s \circ t \circ s$ (b) $s \circ s \circ s \circ t \circ s \circ s \circ s \circ s$ (c) $t \circ t \circ s \circ s \circ t \circ t \circ s$

A5 What is special about each of these?

(a) $s \circ t \circ s \circ s \circ t \circ s$ (b) $s \circ t \circ t \circ t \circ s \circ t$ (c) $s \circ s \circ s \circ t \circ s \circ s \circ s \circ t$

If you do $s \circ s \circ s \circ t \circ s \circ s \circ s \circ s \circ t$ you will finish up in exactly the same position as you started in.
So the combination $s \circ s \circ s \circ t \circ s \circ s \circ s \circ s \circ t$ has the same effect as doing nothing.
It is useful to have a special symbol for 'do nothing'.
We shall use i (for **identity**). So we can write

$$s \circ s \circ s \circ t \circ s \circ s \circ s \circ s \circ t = i$$

A6 Explain why $s \circ t \circ s \circ t$ is equal to i, but $s \circ t \circ s$ is not equal to i.

A7 Using t's only, write down two combinations which are each equal to i.

A8 What is the simplest combination equal to $s \circ t \circ s$?

Simplifying

Here is a combination of moves.

$$s \circ s \circ s \circ t \circ s \circ s \circ t \circ s \circ s \circ s \circ t \circ t \circ s \circ s \circ s \circ s \circ t \circ s$$

We can find a simpler combination equal to this one without using a marker and doing every move.

We use the facts that $t \circ t$ is equal to i
and $s \circ t \circ s$ is equal to t.
This is how it is done.

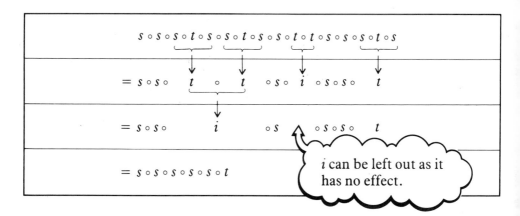

A9 Simplify each of these.

(a) $s \circ t \circ s \circ s \circ t$

(b) $t \circ s \circ t \circ s \circ t \circ t$

(c) $s \circ s \circ t \circ s \circ t$

(d) $s \circ t \circ s \circ s \circ t \circ s \circ s \circ s \circ t \circ s \circ s \circ s \circ t \circ t \circ s$

(e) $t \circ s \circ s \circ s \circ t \circ s \circ s \circ t \circ t \circ t \circ s \circ s \circ t \circ s \circ t$

(f) $s \circ t \circ s \circ t \circ s \circ s \circ s \circ t \circ s \circ s \circ s \circ t \circ s \circ s$

B Three cubes

In the previous section, you were doing a novel kind of algebra,
in which letters stood for moves.
In this section, letters are used to stand for ways of re-arranging
a group of objects.

Three cubes are placed in a pile.

One kind of move is allowed. It is
'move the bottom cube to the top'.
This move will be called p.

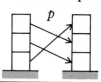

To see what happens when p is
done twice, we letter the starting
position of the cubes.

The double move shown here is
$p \circ p$ (p followed by p).

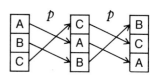

$p \circ p$ has the same effect as
this single move.

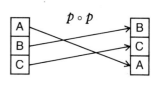

B1 Describe in words the single move equivalent to $p \circ p$.

B2 (a) Draw a diagram to show what happens when you do $p \circ p \circ p$.
Letter the starting position as above.

(b) Draw an arrow diagram for the single move equivalent to $p \circ p \circ p$.

(c) What single move is equivalent to $p \circ p \circ p \circ p$?

B3 Explain why it is impossible to get from $\begin{matrix} A \\ B \\ C \end{matrix}$ to $\begin{matrix} B \\ A \\ C \end{matrix}$ using only move p
(any number of times).

Now we introduce a new move q.

q means 'swap the positions of the top two cubes'.

We can now investigate combinations of p and q, for example, $p \circ q$, $q \circ p$, $p \circ p \circ q$, and so on.

B4 Can you get from $\begin{smallmatrix} A \\ B \\ C \end{smallmatrix}$ to $\begin{smallmatrix} C \\ B \\ A \end{smallmatrix}$ using some combination of p and q?

If so, write down the combination you use.

B5 Starting with the cubes lettered $\begin{smallmatrix} A \\ B \\ C \end{smallmatrix}$, see how many different

positions you can get using p's, q's or both.
Are there any positions you cannot get?

B6 Is $p \circ q$ equal to $q \circ p$?

B7 (a) How would you describe $p \circ q \circ p \circ q$?

(b) Is $p \circ q \circ p \circ q$ equal to $q \circ p \circ q \circ p$?

Challenge questions

B8 Find a set of rules for simplifying combinations such as

$$p \circ p \circ q \circ p \circ q \circ p \circ q \circ q \circ p \circ q \circ p.$$

Try your rules out on some combinations of your own.

B9 Now have four cubes instead of three.
p and q have the same descriptions as before.

Letter the starting position ABCD and see how many different positions you can get using combinations of p, q or both.

C An equilateral triangle

This diagram shows an equilateral triangle with its 3 lines of reflection symmetry and its centre of rotation symmetry.

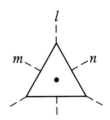

There are six moves we can make which leave the triangle occupying the same space on the page.
Note that the lines l, m and n stay fixed on the page.

L: reflect in the line l.

This interchanges the bottom corners.

M: reflect in the line m.

This interchanges the top corner and the bottom left-hand corner.

N: reflect in the line n.

This interchanges the top corner and the bottom right-hand corner.

P: rotate 120° clockwise.

This moves each corner one place clockwise.

Q: rotate 120° anticlockwise.

This moves each corner one place anticlockwise.

I: the identity.

This leaves every corner where it was before.

To see the effect of combining the moves, it is useful to mark the corners of the triangle in its starting position.

This diagram shows L∘P (L followed by P).

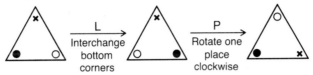

The overall effect of L∘P is to interchange the top corner and the bottom right-hand corner.

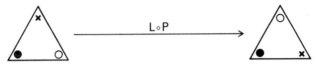

So L∘P is equivalent to N. We write this L∘P = N.

C1 Draw diagrams like the first one above for each of these combinations. Write down the single move equivalent to each combination.

(a) P∘L   (b) Q∘I   (c) L∘M

C2 A useful way of recording the effects of combinations of two moves is a table.

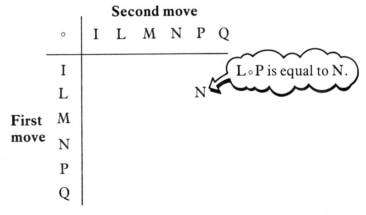

	Second move					
∘	I	L	M	N	P	Q
I						
L				N		
M						
N						
P						
Q						

L∘P is equal to N.

Copy the table and complete it.

If you do P followed by Q, it is easy to see that you
end up in the same position as you started in. So P∘Q = I.

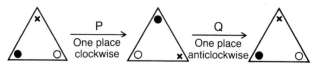

A move which 'undoes' another move is called its **inverse**.
We say Q is the inverse of P.

C3 What is the inverse of   (a) Q   (b) L

A move which is its own inverse is called a **self-inverse** move.

C4 Which of the moves are self-inverse?

Every combination of moves can be reduced to a single move which
has the same effect. Here is an example.

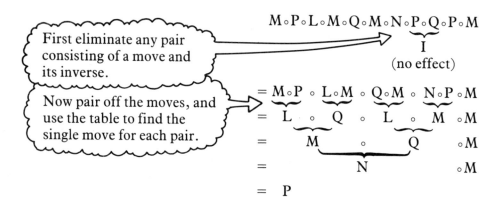

C5 Reduce each of these to a single move.

(a) P∘P∘M∘N∘N∘P∘M∘M∘Q

(b) Q∘P∘M∘M∘L∘M∘N∘P∘L

(c) L∘M∘Q∘P∘L∘P∘Q∘M∘N

(d) M∘N∘L∘P∘Q∘M∘Q

D Three coins

Place three coins in a row, all with tails upwards.

Suppose two moves are allowed. Call them l and r.

l means 'turn over the two left-hand coins'.

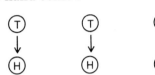

r means 'turn over the two right-hand coins'.

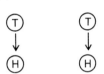

D1 What happens if you do (a) $l \circ l$ (b) $r \circ r$

D2 (a) Describe in words the effect of $l \circ r$.

(b) Is $r \circ l$ equal to $l \circ r$?

(c) What can you say about $r \circ l \circ r$?

(d) What can you say about $l \circ r \circ l$?

Let s stand for the move 'turn the outer pair of coins over'.

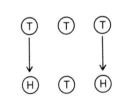

D3 Make a combination table for i, l, r and s.

$\circ$	i	l	r	s
i				
l				
r				
s				

D4 r^3 is a short way of writing $r \circ r \circ r$.
What single move is equivalent to (a) r^3 (b) l^4 (c) s^3
(d) r^7 (e) s^{23} (f) l^{101} (g) $s^{17} \circ l^{28}$ (h) $r^{854} \circ l^{507} \circ s^{1024}$

E Generators

Section B was about arranging three cubes in a pile.
There are six different moves which can be made.

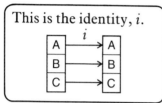 This is the identity, *i*.

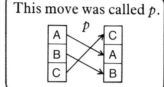 This move was called *p*.

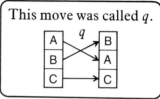 This move was called *q*.

The other three moves can all be described using only *p* and *q*.

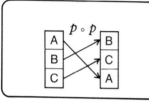

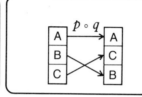

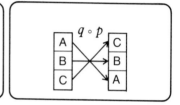

We say that *p* and *q* **generate** all the moves.

E1 Look back at your results in section D (three coins).
It is not possible to generate all possible ways of turning
over the coins using only combinations of moves *l* and *r*.

There are four moves which cannot be generated using
combinations of *l* and *r*. Describe them in words.

Test a friend sometime.

Put three coins on a table with tails up.
Ask your friend to get three heads up by
turning the coins over two at a time.

36

The equilateral triangle

In section C, we saw that there are six moves which leave an equilateral triangle occupying the same space on a page. We called these six moves I, L, M, N, P and Q.

An interesting question is this: what is the smallest number of moves needed to generate the rest?

You may find your combination table from section C useful in answering the next question.

E2 (a) Is there one move which can be used to generate the rest? (If it was L, for example, then all the other moves would have to be combinations of L only: $L \circ L$, $L \circ L \circ L$, and so on.)

(b) Explain why the two rotations, P and Q, cannot be combined to generate the other moves.

(c) Find out whether L and M will generate all the other moves. (For example, $L \circ M = Q$.)

(d) In (c) you used two reflections, L and M. Investigate whether it is possible to generate all the moves using one reflection and one rotation.

The square

There are eight moves which leave a square occupying the same space on the page.

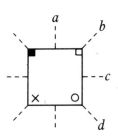

E3 Make a list of the eight moves.

E4 Suppose you have only these two moves.

A: reflect in line a.

B: reflect in line b.

Try to generate, using A and B, the move C: 'reflect in line c'.
It may help to cut out a square and mark the corners (both sides) as shown.

If we start with 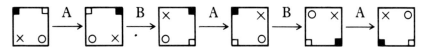, then move C takes us to [figure].

One way to generate C using A and B is this:

[figure sequence: A, B, A, B, A]

So A∘B∘A∘B∘A = C. (There is a simpler way, too.)

E5 Let H be the move 'rotate 180°'.

So H takes  to [figure].

(a) Draw a diagram to show how H can be generated using A and B.

Show how each of these can be generated from A and B.

(b) P: rotate 90° clockwise (c) Q: rotate 90° anticlockwise

(d) D: reflect in line *d* (e) I: the identity

(f) Explain why the two reflections A and C will **not** generate all the other moves.

E6 Which of the eight moves are not self-inverse?

E7 (optional)
There are ten moves which leave a regular pentagon occupying the same space as before.

(a) Make a list of them.

(b) Find the minimum number of moves which will generate all the rest.
Draw diagrams to show how it can be done.

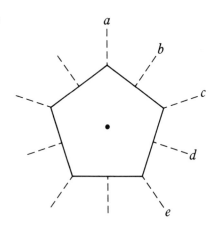

F Moves on a grid

Suppose the two moves shown here
are the only two kinds of move
allowed on a grid.

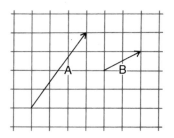

If we start at $(0, 0)$ and do $A \circ B$
(A followed by B), we finish at $(5, 5)$.

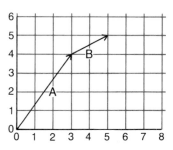

F1 (a) If you start at $(0, 0)$ and do $B \circ A$, where do you finish?

(b) Is $B \circ A$ equal to $A \circ B$?

F2 Starting at $(0, 0)$, find the finishing point for each of these
combinations of moves.

(a) $A \circ A \circ A$

(b) $A \circ B \circ A$

(c) $A \circ B \circ A \circ B$

(d) $A \circ A \circ B \circ A \circ A$

(e) $B \circ B \circ B \circ A \circ B \circ B$

(f) $B \circ B \circ B \circ B$

F3 Write down a combination of A and B which will
take you from $(0, 0)$ to each of these points.
(a) $(16, 8)$ (b) $(15, 10)$ (c) $(8, 9)$ (d) $(10, 12)$

You may have met moves like A and B before.
They are called **vectors** and are often represented by
small letters with squiggles under them: $\underset{\sim}{a}$, $\underset{\sim}{b}$.

Instead of $\underset{\sim}{a} \circ \underset{\sim}{b}$ ('$\underset{\sim}{a}$ followed by $\underset{\sim}{b}$') we write $\underset{\sim}{a} + \underset{\sim}{b}$.

Vectors can be described by a pair of numbers written
in a column in square brackets, like this.

$$\underset{\sim}{a} = \begin{bmatrix} 3 \\ 4 \end{bmatrix} \begin{array}{l} \text{3 units across, left to right} \\ \text{4 units up} \end{array}$$

Let $\underset{\sim}{r} = \begin{bmatrix} 3 \\ 1 \end{bmatrix}$ and $\underset{\sim}{s} = \begin{bmatrix} 2 \\ 3 \end{bmatrix}$.

We can use $\underset{\sim}{r}$ and $\underset{\sim}{s}$ to generate
other vectors.

For example,

$$\underset{\sim}{r} + \underset{\sim}{r} + \underset{\sim}{r} + \underset{\sim}{s} = \begin{bmatrix} 11 \\ 6 \end{bmatrix}.$$

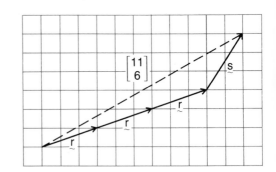

F4 Find combinations of $\underset{\sim}{r}$ and $\underset{\sim}{s}$ which give these vectors.

(a) $\begin{bmatrix} 13 \\ 9 \end{bmatrix}$ (b) $\begin{bmatrix} 18 \\ 6 \end{bmatrix}$ (c) $\begin{bmatrix} 17 \\ 8 \end{bmatrix}$ (d) $\begin{bmatrix} 13 \\ 16 \end{bmatrix}$

F5 Draw a grid with axes numbered from $^-15$ to 15.
Ring all the points which can be reached from (0, 0) by
combinations of $\underset{\sim}{r}$ and $\underset{\sim}{s}$. (Keep the grid for later.)

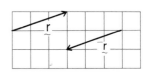

$^-\underset{\sim}{r}$ stands for a vector of the same length
as $\underset{\sim}{r}$, but in the opposite direction. So $^-\underset{\sim}{r} = \begin{bmatrix} ^-3 \\ ^-1 \end{bmatrix}$.

When you combine $\underset{\sim}{r}$ and $^-\underset{\sim}{r}$, you get back to your
starting point. So $\underset{\sim}{r} + {}^-\underset{\sim}{r}$ is equivalent to the **identity**.

$$\begin{bmatrix} 3 \\ 1 \end{bmatrix} + \begin{bmatrix} ^-3 \\ ^-1 \end{bmatrix} = \begin{bmatrix} 0 \\ 0 \end{bmatrix} \quad \text{This is the identity.}$$

So $^-\underset{\sim}{r}$ is the **inverse** of $\underset{\sim}{r}$.

F6 (a) Write down the column vector for the inverse of s̰.

(b) Show how each of these vectors can be generated by a combination of r̰ and ⁻s̰.

(i) $\begin{bmatrix} 1 \\ -2 \end{bmatrix}$ (ii) $\begin{bmatrix} 2 \\ -4 \end{bmatrix}$ (iii) $\begin{bmatrix} 4 \\ -1 \end{bmatrix}$ (iv) $\begin{bmatrix} -1 \\ -5 \end{bmatrix}$ (v) $\begin{bmatrix} 10 \\ 1 \end{bmatrix}$

F7 On the grid you drew for question F5, put a cross on every point which can be reached from $(0, 0)$ using combinations of r̰, ⁻r̰, s̰, ⁻s̰.

F8 Suppose you want to get from $(0, 0)$ to any point with positive whole-number coordinates, by using combinations of just **two** vectors. Which two vectors would you choose?

G Ordinary arithmetic

The ideas of **identity** and **inverse** can also be used with numbers (positive and negative).

G1 If we are thinking of **addition**, the identity would be a number which when added to any number leaves that number unchanged.

So if a stands for any number, and i stands for the identity, then $a + i$ must always be equal to a.

What number must i stand for?

G2 Take the number 3. Its **inverse** is the number you have to add to 3 to get the identity i.

(a) What is the inverse of 3?

(b) What is the inverse of 7?

(c) What is the inverse of ⁻2?

Because we have been thinking about addition, the identity is called the **additive identity** and the inverse of a number is called its **additive inverse**.

The additive identity is 0. The additive inverse of, say, 3 is ⁻3.

G3 If we are thinking of **multiplication**, the **multificative identity** would be a number which, when multiplied by any number, leaves that number unchanged.

So if a stands for any number and j stands for the multiplicative identity, then $a \times j$ must always be equal to a.

What number does j stand for?

G4 Take the number 5. Its **multiplicative inverse** is the number you have to multiply 5 by to get the identity j.

(a) What is the multiplicative inverse of 5?

(b) What is the multiplicative inverse of 8?

(c) What is the multiplicative inverse of $\frac{1}{2}$?

G5 Which number has no multiplicative inverse?

G6 (a) What do we call the numbers which can be generated using only the number 2 and addition?

(b) Which number can be used to generate by addition all positive whole numbers?

(c) What two numbers can be used to generate by addition all positive and negative whole numbers?

(d) Investigate what other pairs of numbers can be used to generate by addition all positive and negative numbers.

G7 In chapter 1 you met arithmetic modulo 7. Here is its multiplication table.

(a) What is the multiplicative identity?

(b) What is the multiplicative inverse of
(i) 2 (ii) 3 (iii) 4 (iv) 5 (v) 6

×	0	1	2	3	4	5	6
0	0	0	0	0	0	0	0
1	0	1	2	3	4	5	6
2	0	2	4	6	1	3	5
3	0	3	6	2	5	1	4
4	0	4	1	5	2	6	3
5	0	5	3	1	6	4	2
6	0	6	5	4	3	2	1

Problems and investigations (2)

1   This tree is made from 5 metal links of equal length.

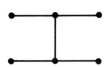

There are many ways in which this tree can be put down on a flat surface (and still be a tree).

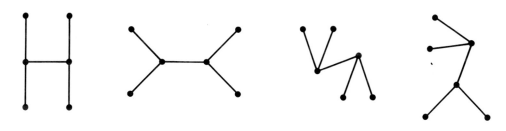

We will think of all these trees as being really the same tree.

This tree, however, is a different tree. Although it too is made from 5 links, it cannot be put down on a flat surface so as to look like the previous tree.

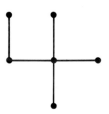

How many other different trees can be made with the 5 links? To start you off, here is one which is different from both of the previous trees.

How many different trees can be made with 6 links? 7 links?

2 A robot moves around on triangular spotty paper.

The position of the robot is shown by ⊙.

The arrow shows the direction in which it is facing.

The robot can make two kinds of move:

f means 'move forward 1 unit'.

r means 'rotate 60° clockwise'.

The symbol ∘ means 'followed by'.

In the diagram on the right the robot has made the move

$$f \circ r \circ r \circ f$$

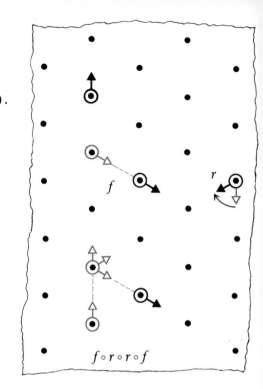

(a) Write down each of these moves as a combination of *f* and *r*.

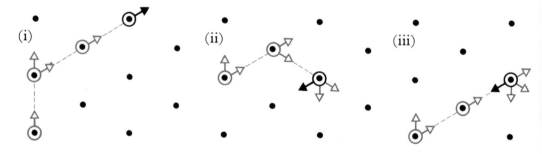

(i) (ii) (iii)

(b) Draw a diagram for each of these moves

(i) *r* ∘ *f* ∘ *r* ∘ *f* (ii) *f* ∘ *r* ∘ *f* ∘ *r*

(c) Verify that the combination *f* ∘ *r* ∘ *f* ∘ *r* ∘ *f* ∘ *r* ∘ *f* ∘ *r* ∘ *f* ∘ *r* ∘ *f* ∘ *r* ∘ *f*
makes the robot end up in the same position as it starts in.

Find as many other combinations as you can, involving up to six *f*s and up to six *r*s, which make the robot end up in its starting position.

44

4 Networks and polyhedra

A Networks: a check-up

A1 This diagram shows a network.

(a) What are the points A, B, C, D and E called?

(b) What are the lines AB, AC, and so on, called?

(c) What is the degree of D?

(d) What is the degree of E?

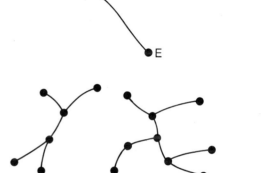

A2 (a) What special name do these networks have?

(b) What is special about them?

A3 A network has four vertices, whose degrees are 3, 3, 5, 1. How can you work out the number of edges without drawing the network?

A4 A network has seven vertices, all of degree 4. How many edges does it have?

The answers to these questions are to be found in the earlier chapter on networks.

A1: see page 19.   A2: see page 23.

A3, A4: see page 22.

B Regions

All the networks in this chapter will be **planar**.
This means they lie in a plane, so no edges cross over one another.

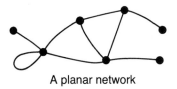

A planar network

A non-planar network

The edges of a planar network split up the plane in which the network lies into **regions**.

The network on the right has 5 regions.
Region 5 is the **outside region** (the region outside the network).

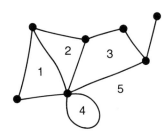

B1 How many regions does each of these networks have?
Do not forget to include the outside region in each case.

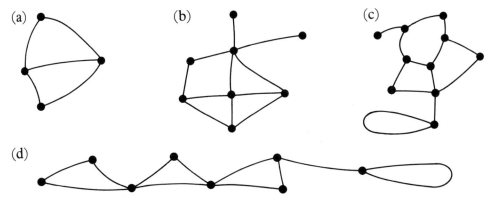

B2 Draw a tree.
How many regions does it have?

Is it the same number for any tree?

B3 Make a table, like this.

Number of vertices	Number of regions	Number of edges

(a) Count the vertices, regions and edges in each network below.
Don't forget the outside region in each one!

Write the numbers for each network in your table.

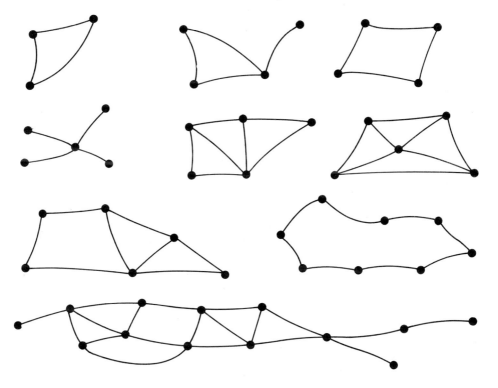

(b) Draw some more networks of your own.
Count the vertices, regions and edges and write the
numbers in your table.

(c) Find a rule connecting the numbers of vertices, regions
and edges in a network.
Get your answer checked before you continue.

47

C Polyhedra

Later in this chapter we shall see the reason for the rule connecting the numbers of vertices, regions and edges of a network.

In this section, we shall find that there is a similar rule for **polyhedra**. A polyhedron is a solid with flat, or **plane**, faces.

'Polyhedron' is Greek for 'many faces'.

Here are some examples of polyhedra.
Some have special names.

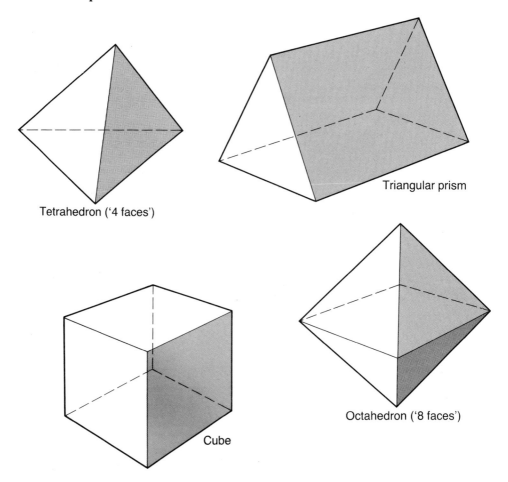

Tetrahedron ('4 faces')

Triangular prism

Cube

Octahedron ('8 faces')

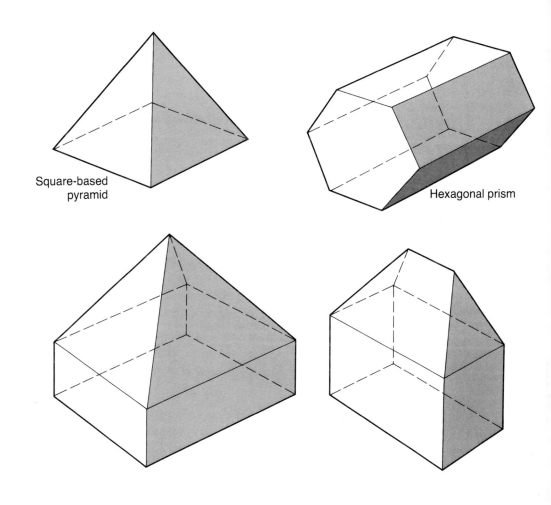

Square-based pyramid

Hexagonal prism

The corners of a polyhedron are called its **vertices**.
The **edges** are formed where two faces meet.

C1 Count the vertices, the faces and the edges of each
polyhedron shown on these two pages.
Write the numbers in a table.

Find a rule connecting the numbers.

D Schlegel diagrams

This is the rule connecting the numbers of vertices, regions and edges of a network.

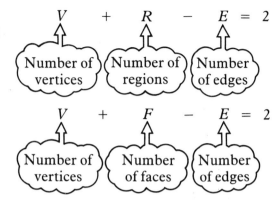

$$V + R - E = 2$$

Number of vertices · Number of regions · Number of edges

This is the rule connecting the number of vertices, faces and edges of a polyhedron.

$$V + F - E = 2$$

Number of vertices · Number of faces · Number of edges

These rules are called **Euler's rules**, after the 18th century Swiss mathematician Euler (pronounced 'Oiler').

The rules are very similar, and there is a reason for this. It is because every polyhedron can be converted into a planar network. The pictures below show how it can be done for a cube.

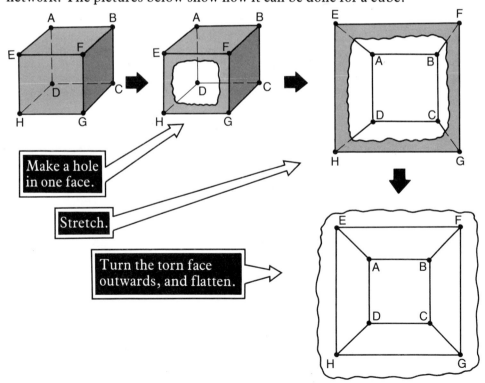

Make a hole in one face.

Stretch.

Turn the torn face outwards, and flatten.

This network is called the **Schlegel diagram** for a cube. (Say 'Shlay-gell'.)

Each region, **including the outside**, corresponds to a face of the cube.

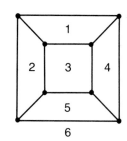

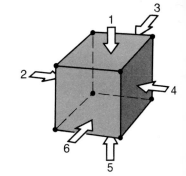

D1 There are two possible Schlegel diagrams for a triangular prism. Copy both of them and letter their vertices correctly.

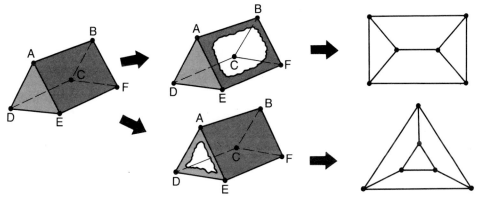

D2 Draw a Schlegel diagram for this tetrahedron, by thinking of the face ABC as 'opened out'.

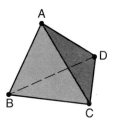

D3 Draw two Schlegel diagrams for this square-based pyramid,

(a) by opening out the square QRST

(b) by opening out the triangle PQR

Check that the number of regions is correct, and that each region has the correct number of edges.

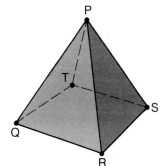

E Euler's rules: the reason why

Euler's rules are: for networks, $V + R - E = 2$,
                     for polyhedra, $V + F - E = 2$.

These two rules are really the same, because every polyhedron can be converted into a network by means of a Schlegel diagram. Each **face** of the polyhedron becomes a **region**.

So we only need to explain why the rule is true for networks.

We start by assuming that **every network can be built up edge by edge, starting from a single vertex and no edges.**

Here is an example of a network being built up from a single vertex. A **new edge** is added at each stage. The table shows the values of V, R, E and $V + R - E$ at each stage.

	V	R	E	$V + R - E$
	1	1	0	2
	2	1	1	2
	3	1	2	2
	3	2	3	2
	4	2	4	2
	4	3	5	2

E1   Study the table carefully. Make a similar table for each of these networks.

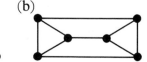

(a)   (b)

Now we can explain why $V + R - E$ will always be 2 for any planar network.

When you start with a single vertex, V is 1 to start with.
R is 1 (the outside region) and E is 0.

So $V + R - E$ is 2 to start with.

Think back to the tables you made for question E1.
There are two ways in which a new edge can be added to a network.

(1) You can add a new **vertex** at the same time, like this, for example.

When you do this, then V and E both go up by 1, and R stays the same.
So $V + R - E$ is unchanged.

(2) The other way to add an edge is to join one existing vertex to another (or to itself). When you do this you make a new **region**.

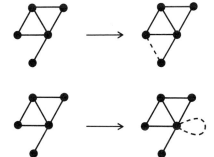

Here R and E both go up by 1, and V stays the same.
So $V + R - E$ is unchanged.

$V + R - E$ is 2 to start with.
Its value is not changed as the network is built up edge by edge.

So it must always be 2.

F Using Euler's rule

The **degree** of a vertex of a polyhedron means the same as in the case of a network. It is the number of half-edges which meet there.

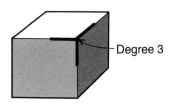
Degree 3

Euler's rule can be used to calculate the value of one of the letters V, F and E when the values of the other two are known.

For example, if V is 7 and F is 3, then E can be calculated, like this.

$$V + F - E = 2$$
$$7 + 3 - E = 2$$
$$10 - E = 2$$
$$E = 8$$

F1 (a) Calculate F when $V = 10$ and $E = 24$.

(b) Calculate V when $F = 16$ and $E = 30$.

Suppose a polyhedron has 10 vertices each of degree 3. Then the total number of **half-edges** must be $10 \times 3 = \mathbf{30}$ (because each vertex has 3 half-edges meeting at it).

So the total number of edges must be **15**.

Now we can calculate the number of faces, like this.

$$V + F - E = 2$$
$$10 + F - 15 = 2$$
$$F - 5 = 2$$
$$F = 7$$

F2 A polyhedron has 6 vertices each of degree 4.

(a) Calculate the number of edges.

(b) Calculate the number of faces.

(c) Which of the polyhedra on pages 48 and 49 fits this description?

F3 A polyhedron has 6 vertices each of degree 3.
Calculate its number of faces.

F4 Calculate the number of faces of a polyhedron which has
20 vertices each of degree 3.

F5 How many faces does a polyhedron have if it has 7 vertices,
4 being of degree 3 and 3 being of degree 4?

These shapes can be fixed together
to make a polyhedron.

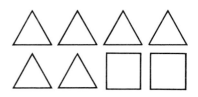

Every side of a shape pairs off with
a side of one of the other shapes
to make an edge of the polyhedron.

The 6 triangles have 18 sides altogether,
and the 2 squares have 8 sides.
That makes 26 sides in all.

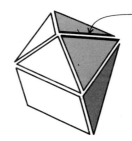

The sides of
the faces
pair off to
make edges.

The sides pair off to make edges, so
the number of edges must be $\frac{26}{2} = 13$.

F6 A polyhedron has 10 triangular faces.

(a) How many edges does it have?

(b) Use Euler's rule to calculate the number of vertices.

F7 How many vertices does a polyhedron have if it has
10 faces, all of them 4-sided?

F8 Explain why a polyhedron cannot have 5 faces, all
of them being triangles.

F9 A polyhedron has five triangular faces and three 5-sided faces.
Calculate the number of vertices of the polyhedron.

G Regular polyhedra

In a **regular** polyhedron, every face has the same number of sides, and every vertex has the same degree.

We can use algebra to find out what kinds of regular polyhedron there are.

The simplest kind of face is a triangle and the simplest kind of vertex is a vertex of degree 3.

So to start with suppose a regular polyhedron has every face a triangle and every vertex of degree 3.

1	Use a letter to stand for the unknown number of faces.	Let n be the number of faces.
2	Each face has 3 sides. Find the total number of sides.	Number of sides $= n \times 3 = 3n$.
3	Each edge is made from 2 sides. Find the number of edges.	Number of edges $= \dfrac{3n}{2} = 1\tfrac{1}{2}n$
4	Now we need the number of vertices. Each vertex is of degree 3, so 3 half-edges meet at each one.	
	So we find the number of half-edges. (Each edge makes 2 half-edges.)	Number of $\tfrac{1}{2}$-edges $= 1\tfrac{1}{2}n \times 2$ $= 3n$
	And then we divide by 3 to get the number of vertices (because 3 half-edges meet at each vertex).	Number of vertices $= \dfrac{3n}{3} = n$
5	Now we have expressions for F, E and V.	$F = n, \quad E = 1\tfrac{1}{2}n, \quad V = n$
	We can write down Euler's rule.	$V + F - E = 2$
	And we can replace V, F and E by their expressions. We get an equation to solve.	$n + n - 1\tfrac{1}{2}n = 2$

6 We solve the equation.	$n + n - 1\frac{1}{2}n = 2$
	$2n \quad - 1\frac{1}{2}n = 2$
	$\frac{1}{2}n = 2$
	$n = 4$

7 Now we go back to the expressions for F, E and V in step 5.	$F = n = \mathbf{4}$ $\qquad$ $E = 1\frac{1}{2}n = \mathbf{6}$
	$V = n = \mathbf{4}$

So if every face of a polyhedron is a triangle and every vertex is of degree 3, there must be 4 vertices, 6 edges and 4 faces.

This regular polyhedron is a **regular tetrahedron.**

G1 Suppose every face of a polyhedron is a triangle and every vertex is of degree 4.
Write out the working to find V, E and F as in the right-hand sides of panels 1 to 7.

What is this regular polyhedron called?

G2 Suppose every face is a triangle and every vertex is of degree 5. Find V, E and F as before.

G3 Suppose every face is a triangle and every vertex is of degree 6. See what happens when you work out V, E and F. Can you explain it?

G4 See what happens if you suppose every face is a triangle and every vertex is of degree 7.

G5 Work out V, E and F for each of these. (Some are impossible.)

	Number of sides of each face	Degree of each vertex
(a)	4	3
(b)	4	4
(c)	5	3
(d)	5	4
(e)	6	3

So far you should have found four more regular polyhedra apart from the regular tetrahedron, making five in all.

These five are the only regular polyhedra there are.

Regular polyhedron		V	F	E
Regular tetrahedron		4	4	6
Regular octahedron		6	8	12
Cube		8	6	12
Regular dodecahedron		20	12	30
Regular icosahedron		12	20	30

Look at the values of V, F and E for an octahedron and compare them with the values for a cube.
The values of V and F are interchanged and the value of E is the same.

Each of these two polyhedra is called the **dual** of the other.
If we start with an octahedron, put a vertex at the centre of each face and then join up these vertices, we get a cube.
Similarly the other way round.

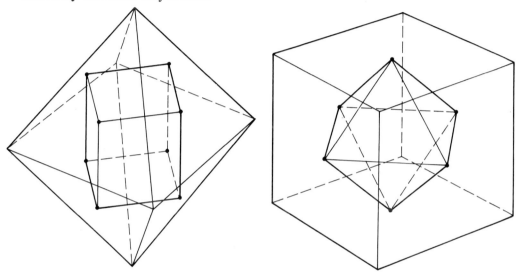

G6 What is the dual of (a) a regular dodecahedron
(b) a regular icosahedron (c) a regular tetrahedron

G7 Every polyhedron has a dual.
This diagram shows the dual of
a triangular prism.

Sketch these polyhedra with
their duals. Write down the
values of V, F and E for each
polyhedron and its dual.

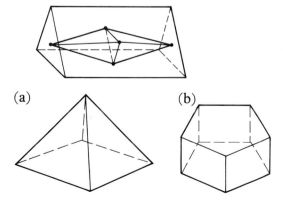

(a)

(b)

H Problems on polyhedra

Do these questions by calculation using Euler's rule, and algebra if necessary.

H1 A polyhedron has 7 faces. 4 of them are pentagons and 3 of them are quadrilaterals.

(a) How many edges does this polyhedron have?

(b) How many vertices does it have?

H2 A rhombic dodecahedron has 12 identical faces, all of them rhombuses.

(a) How many edges does it have?

(b) How many vertices?

(c) Explain why it is impossible for the degree of every vertex to be the same.

H3 A polyhedron has 2 hexagonal (6-sided) faces, and all its other faces are triangles.
Let the number of triangular faces be t.

(a) Write down an expression for the total number of sides in all the faces of the polyhedron.

(b) Write down an expression for the number of edges of the polyhedron.

(c) Use Euler's rule to write down an expression for the number of vertices.

(d) If each vertex is of degree 4, write down an expression for the number of half-edges.

(e) From your answer to (d) write down an expression for the number of edges.

(f) In your answers to (b) and (e) you have two expressions for the number of edges. Put them equal and calculate the value of t.

5 In your mind's eye

The problems in this chapter can quite easily be solved by making models. But that is not the point. Can you solve them by **thinking** alone, seeing the objects 'in your mind's eye'?

1 This is a 'net' of a cube. (If it is cut out, folded and stuck together it will make a cube.)

The triangle is to be cut out. Another triangle of the same shape and size is to be cut out of the face opposite this one, so that the two triangular 'windows' will match up opposite each other.

Draw the net with both triangles in place.

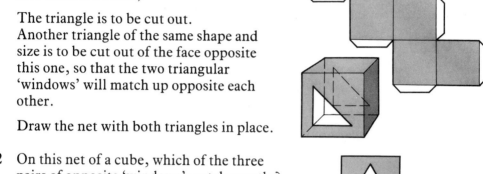

2 On this net of a cube, which of the three pairs of opposite 'windows' match exactly?

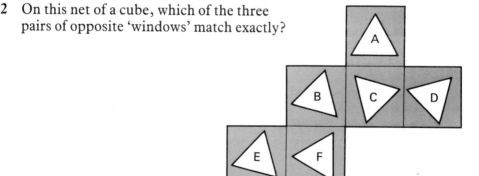

3 | Object A is made from 7 cubes. | Which of these are pictures of object A? |

4 This slab is made from square tiles stuck together. Each tile is the same colour on the top and on the bottom.

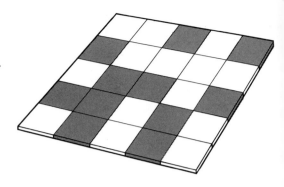

(a) Which of these are pictures of the other side of the slab?

A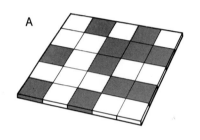

B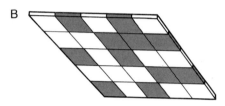

C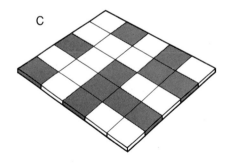

D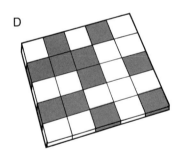

(b) Copy and complete this view of the other side of the slab.

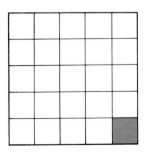

5 If you slice a cube by a plane through the four points marked here, what is the shape of the cross-section?

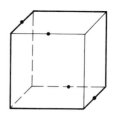

6 Five dice are made, all to this pattern.

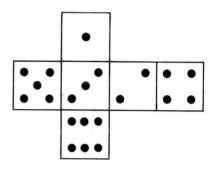

The five dice are glued to each other, so that **faces glued together have the same number on them**. The result is a shape like this.

This is another view of the same shape. Only one of the visible faces has been marked.

Copy the diagram and mark all the other visible faces correctly.

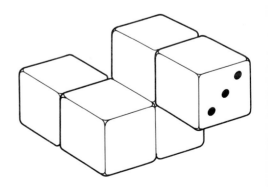

7 If you cut out this shape, fold all dotted lines up and all solid lines down, and stick the lettered pieces back to back (a to A, and so on), what framework will you get?

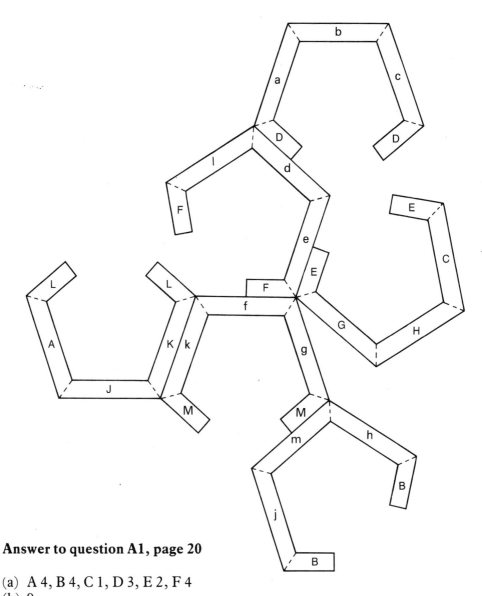

Answer to question A1, page 20

(a) A 4, B 4, C 1, D 3, E 2, F 4
(b) 9